New & Selected Poems

ALSO BY IAN DAVIDSON

By Tiny Twisting Ways (Aquifer 2021)
From a Council House in Connacht (Oystercatcher 2021)
On the Way to Work (Shearsman Books, 2017)
Gateshead and Back (Crater 2017)
In Agitation (KFS 2014)
The Tyne and Wear Poems (Red Squirrel Press, 2014)
Into Thick Hair (Wild Honey Press, 2010)
Partly in Riga (Shearsman Books, 2010)
Familiarity Breeds (Oystercatcher, 2008)
As if Only (Shearsman Books, 2007)
Dark Wires (West House Books, 2007) *with Zoë Skoulding*
No Way Back (West House Books, 2004)
At a Stretch (Shearsman Books, 2004)
Harsh (Spectacular Diseases, 2003)
Human Remains and Sudden Movements (West House Books, 2003)
Wipe Out (Short Run, 1995)
Human to Begin With (Poetical Histories, 1991)
The Patrick Poems (Amra, 1991)
No Passage Landward (Open Township, 1989)
It is Now as it was Then (Mica Press/Actual Size, 1983 *with John Muckle*

Ian Davidson

New and Selected Poems

Shearsman Books

First published in the United Kingdom in 2022 by
Shearsman Books
P O Box 4239
Swindon
SN3 9FN

Shearsman Books Ltd Registered Office
30–31 St. James Place, Mangotsfield, Bristol BS16 9JB
(this address not for correspondence)

www.shearsman.com

ISBN 978-1-84861-826-8

Copyright © Ian Davidson, 2003, 2004, 2007, 2010, 2022.
The right of Ian Davidson to be identified as the author of
this work has been asserted by him in accordance with the
Copyrights, Designs and Patents Act of 1988.
All rights reserved.

Acknowledgments

'Coming and Going' was published in *Plumwood Mountain* Volume 7 Number 2 (2020); *Harsh* was published by Spectacular Diseases (2003); *Human Remains and Sudden Movements* was published by West House Books (2003); *No Way Back* was published by West House Books (2004); *Familiarity Breeds* was published by Oystercatcher (2008); *Into Thick Hair* was published by Wild Honey Press (2010); *At a Stretch* was published by Shearsman Books (2004); *As if Only* was published by Shearsman Books (2007); *Partly in Riga* was published by Shearsman Books (2010).

My sincere thanks to Paul Green of Spectacular Diseases, Alan Halsey and Geraldine Monk of West House Books, Peter Hughes of Oystercatcher, Randolph Healy of Wild Honey Press and Tony Frazer of Shearsman Books for previously publishing the work in these selected poems.

I thank all those publishers and editors who have taken the time and used their money to publish my work. My sincere thanks.

I would also like to thank Ralph Hawkins, John Muckle and Kelvin Corcoran, friends since Essex and without whom my life would have been a lot less.

John Muckle commented on a draft of this book
and I'm grateful for his advice and guidance.

Contents

Coming and Going	9
Harsh	17
Human Remains and Sudden Movements	25
Into Thick Hair	39
At a Stretch	53
As if Only	75
Partly in Riga	89
Appendix	104

*This book is for
Gruffydd, Liam, Cai and Anya.*

Coming and Going

Cuckoo sounds

swallows skim trees

far out at sea waves curl

Crests hanging

Addicted to restriction
in love with lockdown
I tap my arm say, later
as along the way
lambs slither into the world
and begin breathing

The colours of sheep

Wild blue sheep come
down from the commonage
for the summer. Left on rough
pasture at the coast and
easily startled they turn
red and green as
marks of ownership
are slowly added until
they are all colour and
no sheep remains.

In the heat of summer their
heavy coats are worn off the
shoulder or left to hang
on ancient trees and free
of fleece their branding
temporarily absent
the sheep in just their skin
admire themselves
in rivers and pools

or stare deep into
each other's eyes

The song of the hen

With smart red comb and
double yolk the hen can
clear rough ground
and lay eggs, some things
come in packages, the hens
have no fear
a hen can fold her wings and
legs and flatten
as in spatchcock to bathe
in the thin dust that rises

A hen is like a
dinosaur but smarter

Sheet music

The sheet flaps
demanding entry

behind the sheet
the sky a startling blue

Life is like that the
flap of the sheet only
the beginning the
blue sky beckons
the land an
unsolved mystery

The song of the tractor

Coming and going
between holdings,
land defined by
acts of survey and
distribution, acts to
establish an exact price

The song of the landworker

Leaving behind without a
backward glance
our slow walk across
a yard or sodden field
full buckets banging
on our knees
or the weight of
a sack of feed
on our shoulders

Land is not a parcel
passed from hand to hand.
Land is not revealed
with each torn layer.
There is no final prize
on which to feast your eyes.

Land lives in fields,
different every day.
unpredictably

Land gives no guarantees
but springs eternally
clouds bubble up
rain spits, weeds
wither and die

there is nothing like
knowing a
field for ever
in its unreliability

The song of the plasterer

We should have stayed home
and honed language like a
knife blade or a chisel
or given it the weight
of a sledge, or loaded it
onto a hawk to even out
a wall gone haywire,
or spread it so thin that
every grain of sand
impeded the even stroke
where words have a
gritty resistance
between the thin metal blade
and the rough
concrete background

In the wilderness of
teaching and administration,
held back from the
precipitous edge of
thinking,
kept in security and distraction,
tools rust

No way out

The way of the world
is not the highway to the east
but the boreen
at the side of the house that
peters out in the bog

Where John Clare went crazy

Where Patrick Kavanagh cut and ran

Kittens taken too young
become natural born killers
their crazy dichromatic eyes.
like little birds that collect
along the fence,
like clouds on the horizon,
the quad cruising
the boundaries.

Language too will let you down
its ponderous diction,
its second-rate facility.
On land, language
must take its turn.

Song of Itself

So language is a virus so,
readily transmitted and
you is the host
and the orders of syntax
conceal the fertile chaos
of the word, planted
like an idea,
and in the headlong rush
to fill a sentence
words get forgotten
the word and what it is

Words must be
king and queen,
at the points where
farms meet and

fences transmit lambs
looking for fresh pasture
and grass as green as
words that emerge
from the mouths of
babes and weanlings.

Harsh

I

No body is that fit. The divide between spirit on the south bank
and the heady north too long for a single leap. Fat spitting at the
splash back, somebody yells to turn it down, by the lakeside the chariots
swung down low. Just me and her in the restaurant, drawing from memory

on a napkin discarded by a previous diner. Waitress, a personal saviour plan
and serve it on a bed of winter leaves, the full illustration not just the
        bottom line.
The roots of the supper dish deep in the Caribbean potatoes flown in by
special delivery teeth constructed in the back room of a Killarney dental
        practice

moulded to the shape of speech patterns of previous generations.
Cross channel Celtic. Down the familial tubes
genetics squeezed like toothpaste into fresh bodies the wind
carves patterns from the stone the sea washes a little more each storm

tree roots exposed on the shale bank dressed stones in rows
along the tides upper reaches until the orange light sucks.

II

Like a millstone the last remembered thought position of sun, moon and stars.
What parents they were. Blocks of standing stone around which the
          codification
of the spirit world plant and animal in the mechanics of agriculture
and the simple power take off those stormy hills

in the loose bebop prose that slips through the fingers.
Crumpled piles of sodden books heaped against the castle walls.
On a dry day the pages riffle in the wind.
Old estate cars their parents drove

pebbles churned to sand
breakdown of the mind and body.
In the fire of regeneration
do you remember when…?

Recycled paper around a language like the sphinx
the debris of revivalism and the committee for the protection of all stupidity.

III

Deep pools of vowels opening under internal pressure,
the harshness intentional.
On the rank soil leaves bed down.
Near dearth experience

the cat fell while drinking.
Emblazoned across her white chest
the mark of Arthur as around the round
a pit of sibilance, maybe next door banging, westerly

horizontal rain. Wheelbarrow full of dead grammar.
In the scales of blind obsession
tipped by one interest or another
off the three quarter landing, taking its time.

Christmas and couldn't sleep, revellers,
the harshness intentional and local.

IV

Millimetres from a perfect fit the revealed self
develops calluses seals the ends of exposed bone
as it slowly gets its act together.
Tina, get yourself back on the road,

that is the right place for you to be,
stage juddering into place
a fraction at a time.
The intended conversation beneath the

oceans the shifting of tectonic plates
there is nothing better
than to eat and drink, prosper.
The proverbial square peg

fading physics of an unexplored world
intellect clocking on then walking out then settling in to lounge for the night.

V

I groaned and the world tilted it was my head, I couldn't help it
and the heckling from the children lonely in their beds.
Brother. Cuba is a world from which there is no escape
except into slavery. The 4 of Spades as big as a house

the knife blade slides in the slit between the stones and shatters like a horse
into dust an accursed vein of bad blood, oh Incas who held mighty sway and
only allowed visual disturbance as part of an overall plan, rope bridges swing
for the graceless European. She leant towards him, a cigarette between her
        fingers

blowing smoke across his torso the playing card between her eyes
in anticipation of hard work skipping across the rivulets
that drain the marshes into the sea the cheap speed ran out all the stars
flying backwards into space as a microcosm of aspiration.

Things make me nervous, skating across the surface
of sincerity. Drugs, credit card fraud and idleness.

Human Remains
and Sudden Movements

1.

in hot darkness a pool
spreading in the cool morning
water between the banks

drawn across by politics to be
polite here's a way forward
things drifted through

dropped arches fascist
memorabilia a spreading pool
of fact the tall monuments

casting shadows brain
damage from a bulky pinnacle
I can see my house from here a

sphere of influence from holes in the
ground many spikes rise commemorative
and that which has past the industrial

daring the future a series of
rectangles each one over and
under or to one side the fit not

perfect not meant to be people
written over and through the
arch to arch from lighthouse

to lighthouse no more than a heap of
rock where the birds come to roost beyond
the fold around the tides meet

2.

The longitude and the latitude

Within the grid reference the contour lines
leak
between a mountain life is different
higher still no vegetation grows

It sits as if to squat below a certain level
small squares of fields between
dry stone walls we're no goats nor mountain
agiles to climb or needing peace at last

Most sudden movements can cause bruising the
Marxist party or clearing land of its
people for other purposes and that's why the
big house is big and the monument something

to begin at the beginning there is a stretch of
water wider than even my outstretched arms
and spreading across the wooden floor a voice
can go further than that and take up time

3.

Water has less friction I glide on pictures of
water oh choppy sea the superstructure
of pier mighty columns across a
stretch and its failed significance station

Hotel pink flowers against dark stone some potential
difference draws the road through from point to
point whatever pollution they come up with in
layers and slices I heal and clone new bands

And when she smiles, smile, towards sunset
June 18 1815 I am badly drawn and unsure
of coordination what England expects
whether a memory of itself or the real thing

Shadow induced panic the switch thrown across
the face of the earth across the lung the dig
x rayed long held skeletons back by the tide a sea
wall or a tidal wave between the two undertow

4.

the tale of the battered monk
turned out a light well less
an inner courtyard my
architecture is faulty the flexible
spine of the fish and its feathers

washed out to sea on a wave of
optimism back to the wall and
what is it this sand is it blasted
bone or the wall of the cistern
for the wet sacred bones the

sea exhuming out of disinterest for
what angle are they laid at
how does the sun bounce
off the sea the first day all the
grass was bent by a westerly and
when the background is not
granite which splits
evenly down the grain what
material do they use for a cist?

sometimes a one word answer
yes or no an augmented maybe

or the stutter of sources juddering
down the time lines before
lighting up the dark wires
of a brain that's lost its history

a child plays between the cracks
poking a drain with a stick a
hole into somewhere without light
where liquid runs and what is the
shoreline but a barrier why does
digging stop at the high
tide mark the fear of sea
slugs thick kelp a medium

5.

thick with absorbed oxygen the
expertise swims in the brain the
clipboard floats away we classify
the objects in a piece of mind
standing in the air and moving

once dug the ground is never the
same again it's a performance
archaeology of discovering what
really went on or at least as far
as they can tell the real thing

he saw himself pretending to
doubt and that was enough
the queue outside the town hall
spread down the street the projector
was useless with that size of crowd

poetry can be put into words the
purple amongst the marram grass

rain whipped across
a windscreen how a sea shanty feels
from the inside where the mouth of the bay spits in
waves and the jetskis in the jaw
or the curve against the horizon where
the island becomes a wasp waist

on the second day the wind still blew
and the air was full of water, the site
protected from invasion from
young and inexperienced fingers
picking it over disturbing the bones
with the seal of approval others just
worry away at it like the sea washing
through the stone wall or the chapel that
Pennant mapped all the facilities

6.

fractured column to column like a
curtain the fold of the
base stone the road and the railway

weeds grow about the
base indistinguishable
words this close

armour is not ornamental but for
killing the idols of genital
mutilation we stand back and admire

the handiwork nobody
states the obvious
the night sky showing

light until into the early hours
the grass like highlights
in her hair within the dunes

7.

at the bottom of the steps a lighthouse
before coming into daylight the
kittiwakes close enough to

touch the puffins like helicopters inside
a virtual world speed indicates
flying out of the shelter of the cliff then
turning in the wind at some angles

velocity seems terminal sandbags like
maggots on a dead body figures
approaching the chapel on a sand dune
caves such as the Taliban might use to

conceal weaponry what commentary
might a broadsword receive how
deep can a covering be

8.

something to carry around on her front

linen fold
stone ware
concept money

kalashnikov through the doorway
petrol down the vent shaft
mainly pigeons
he shook his angry head

9.

pleats on the chimney pot levelling
the view finder human remains out

of sight of the public skulls crossed
bones petrified forest hair

secret arts of the theodolite different
tracks coalesce patterns coincidence 1.67

stage set the head goes hunting a scale
of human drama income always ready

for increase the walls the edge human
remains the sun shone through his

shaved head wherever I am I'm into
it anyone can fill in a form with

some instruction

10.

around the base of the column

the folds were
continuous

or there are always connections

with so multiple a mortal
diving over and over and
coming up fish or
swimming around the island towing

the great novel anyway
1 or 2 ideas

enough for now

11.

it was possible to see the sea

the interruptions were minimal

where the sun came down
like moving through melting glass
the shape remains

12.

the gap between the sea and the
shore close up
tea turns to dust is
wrapped in 3 cornered bags becomes an
experience mediated through the muslin

take material pulverise it (alcohol breaks
down barriers add water make it art

13.

at the point at which a
monument
hits the ground causing
superficial bruising
a few tree roots torn
shards of

previous civilisations
marbled clay misty
warm water algae
unaccustomed disc trouble
the roots veins the
marbling fat lamb

14.

off the tongue a
spit of land the
test bed less

scientific observation more
dark pooling matter
less metaphor

influence spread like a river bed
no two are ever alike
genes creep forward
she took off her photograph
put up a skeleton
her jaw wired for
I felt pleased
ah felt good

Follow instructions
    1. *shut the door*
    2. *relax*
    3. *as it shall be written*
    4. *awaken*

15.

perspiration formed on his upper lip
he wanted to believe in something good
the form and function of the world
sounds of construction
sounds of agriculture
I lifted mine eyes up to the hills
between Manyana and make
hay a world of difference
weighing the killed pig
sounds of constriction
killing the greased pig

16.

the global breeze
through the bar area
by the lamp light
between ideas
and their execution
the mark of another's hand

shove halfpenny
underlies a relationship
not knowing what money is worth
so much an hour
so it's time
or the unbroken surface of the skin
splitting waves

the in and the out of it

17.

I wrote specifically as if I could do otherwise
the totality escapes me the folds that matter makes up
his brow furrowed its rhyme and reason
at the centre of a cliff a cave at its most
polite I cannot water little becomes more

the door bangs off stage/down beat

with his head in the sand molecules begin to heat up or at the
point of flexing not much alcohol even on Sunday a cigar is
a prick where the sun don't shine all you'll feel is a little prick
he was approaching deaf so the difference between the
sounds of words was barely noticeable and sometimes I

just forget it

what is worth saying
what is worth saving

viable processes a peasant way of life or concrete taking the shape of
whatever it's poured into what he'll do left to his own devices lift
thine eyes up to the hills and trying to get the word order right

lift thine
(fail safe
all your
(never mind
to the hills

Into Thick Hair

Your thick hair extended your
Thin snakeskin trousers or your
Little pill box still pills for-
Gotten taken overseas little
Children cats little kittens

Your thin arms legs their arms thin
Your legs walking embracing
Arms humility brown eyes
Dark hair humbled embracing
Insecurity jealousy

My lower orders your upper
Set cavities some things
Are important enough to
Be worth saying like uppers
And on them the little cats

All ears listening having gone
To bed and lying some things
Are not worth saying under
The covers embracing and
Moments outside and moments

Your knitted mohair jumper
Your green mohair red mohair
Scarlet nylon leggings high heels
Fighting to the death down at
Heel snapped unattached undone

To the death your slashed lipstick
Future face feet drumming wind
Screen all torn canvas sunroof
Sliding against the traffic
Across a junction should have

Stopped there where the signs said halt
Your grey snakeskin shoes animal
Print and design on the surface
Of her skin small hands and feet
Thin veins deep below the skin

Your brown woollen coat uneven
Walk your asymmetrical
Stride the kitten just letting
Go and all ears the baby
Under the tv the volume

Turned up smoke filled rooms
And talking and all those years
And all those years ago talking
And drinking and not talking
Never thought or not thinking

Your boxes full of trinkets
Bits and pieces necklaces
Entwined in necklaces a
Diamond dress ring a jewel
Some old furniture nobody

Wanted or understood hair
Tangled past bracelet so much
To do so little time from
House to house the Chinese
Tower of boxes a cigar

Box a carved wooden box
And old coins from far countries
Tales from the empire a girl's
Adventure story the boxes
Taken out and dishevelled

Hair a slash of lipstick col
Gumming the lashes a tale
Half told colonial
Traces the wild ways beyond
Thought processes or all the

Neurons entangled forgotten
Trinkets tied together with hair
Half remembered images fade
Words mix with other words bits
Tight to her chest bits spilling

Your paintings at all angles
Under the bed your drawings
The bad paintings you carried around
Spilling from their frames out of
Their containers paint thick

As your hair oblivious
To others your pain contained
In unfinished paintings drawn
From all quarters hair pinned up
Smoke curling you weren't always

Although there may have been on
Occasion an anniversary
Or other times when your guard
Was down or the brush angled
Face averted turned away

The trouble with doing some things
Well is you may get the idea
You can do all things well which
Is not necessarily
The case it simply means that

You can do some things well at
The time you do them it is
Not universal truth but
A moment of competence
Amongst many fuck ups never

Assert yourself even on the
Occasions when you may know
What you are doing sustain
A blanket flailing at the
World or attuned to others

Needs be timid in the face
Of the possibility
Of self-confidence a trap
It is only too easy to
Keep your head down bow low scrape

Your hair brain your finger on
The trigger your fast mouth talk
Teeth chattering shock of cold
Dawn light of reason memory
Temporarily on hold

No reason for it at all
The smell of thinking over
Turning over adventures in
The skin trade out of body ex-
Perience special school days

The art of talking without
Thinking immersion under
The influence wine rose to
Neck flushed uncorked spilling from
A well of experience

Springing the slightly crooked
Jawline hair growing inward
The brain wave choking under
Tow rattling on your stony
Shore line brain wave over breaking

Your patience turning over one
Card shrinking columns of cards
The cards shuffle themselves
Onto the piles breaking the
Air slices of bread taken

On the hoof between places
Cards slicing the air between
Images sliced into slices
Chopped up by slow cooking fry
Onions slowly fry chicken

Your Greek holiday your first Greek
Holiday via Berlin maybe
Spain or bulb packing money
Never got to the top of
The list of things to do in

Greece pointing out extra fat
And ingrown hair and naked
On a Greek beach Mailer for
Material a few lines
Of poetry a small sketch

And drinking and talking and not
Thinking too much your Spanish
Holiday the boys under tow
That Greek holiday and the
Water in the tank above

Our heads and drinking wine and
Not talking properly the
Babies came in ones apart
By years the grunt work came in
Spades and years apart and all

That work and loving you trying
To get it right the house right
Food right conversation
Your head in a book you only
Half listening you drunk and not

Listening at all you talking and
Me not listening this is the
Story of a holiday
In Greece via Berlin Munich
The driver passenger the train

Your talking as if it was an
Act that counted for anything
As if it was the same as
Experience itself an
Action like digging painting

Placing words on paper ear
On the rails train approaching
Carriages rattling stuck on the
Tracks and heading east into
The morning into day and light

That was the distant past and
Unaccounted despair
Is ok when there's a future
To be reckoned with a timetable
Like the sea going in and

Out being young and unhappy
Is ok an act that can come
Off and sat alone greedy
For experience blurred
Eyes fading hearing going

The talking going on and
On and a future conjured
Out of thin air and words and
Not what they might mean but how
They arrive ready to hand

Your disappointing hair cuts
Blue cotton suits black trouser
Suits hairdresser unhappy hair
Experiences Mason
Pearson brush tangled ginger

Cat hair sink gummed with hair
And in the 80s woven hair
Swept back from the face and up
From the dented forehead up
To the stormy sky out like a

Wave from the brain another good
Idea gone west then again
Brass neck sophistication
Failing to please under rated cut
Badly unsuited excommun

Icated the pad of ginger
Cat hair carried from house to
House a carrier bag a lock
Of hair a pony tail the
Carrier bags lined up knitting

Never completed unhappy
Endings knit one never make your
Own items of clothing over
And over reiterated
Morning, afternoon and long night

Your something to write about a
Subject a syllable to
Fill up the empty line of
Family handed down from
Mother to child you're something

You are that takes up time in
Quantitative verse the long
Pauses would never do empty
Moments need filling escape
Into the margins at the

End of the line when a click
Clack of discontent an empty
Carriage where sadness should be
Wild despair hair mussed up and
Malcontent devoid of all

Feeling only a few dots where
The empty words might be shut
Down for the night genetic
Material potential
Combinations this content

At a Stretch

From 'The Keokuk Poems'

Cedar Springs

we followed the power lines north
across the money by pass
a small sigh of disappointment
protection behaving badly
many channels of misinformation
little left over, walked
wrote about it

the commercial strip

across crowded rooms within
whatever cost code
they talked until the last minute
scrubbed rows of beach facing seaward
through cloud cover this is America

I take an interest as a percentage
concentrate go for a walk
an industry only ever sustains itself
that's its business

her hair fell across her face
she lifts her arm
oh distant star for listening your soft
obsecenity beyond language
sorry I ever started
borne by many hands
he looked around his
cruise control gone
all hands on deck

someone standing at the queue more
tinned beans beyond the sell by date
like truth by Klein more fries no
wings I flies the Keokuk poems

In Density

1.

when there's money or people
in the question to dispense and
still hanging around or mad

through the window
pale figure sits looks out
figure sits alone sits his money gone

to the four winds money gone
west and now what
water does flow uphill

I know this now I've
rafted I've canoed
there are no firm foundations

when shifting class, chairs
become chains, metal mental
better than thought, suspended

in a state of indecision
between 99 and the full pound
desolate influences, shade of trees

2.

they were young and their Moldavian first class

they were transported in containers
where temporary structures swayed around their heads
arranged to collapse inwards and conceal their bodies
in case of accident

yes sir between the documentary and the film there is an interval which
is not too expensive

free of any reference points
they captured the precise mood

All	The	Way
Free	To	Roam
Fail	Safe	Device
Prince	Of	Peace
For	Love's	Gracious
Hand	To	Mouth
Shut	Da	Fuck
Of	Great	Courage
Go	Back	Home

3.

lessons in abstraction

a big fat zero

a mask of nerve tissue

sailing the ship of capital
foaming at the mouth
until love redeems me

O Xena in your uncanny way
reveal to me my manor

plant life

1.

sand at so much a layer
the foot rested near the head
it's a position
the face sucked in
straightened out
feet outside the curtilage

the site inverted
a monument beaten flat and
wrapped around the globe
from forests tumours eyes
bore holes in the ice, fished out
bruised from all that seeing

in sky and light in
density I camp out wound
down the sedimentary canal along
the towpath I cast in
as far as the I can see
to the socket's extent

shutting down the body parts
plugging in the body parts
exit to port
entering port
sand filled the eye socket
recently disturbed

2.

the statutes of Kilkenny
no breeding with the English
my single strand of blonde
across the attention span
everything, day and night

it was bog standard
a plantation house
its function to become

little possibility of
gaining entry across
loose ground

figure it out

I take the original,
crack it like a chestnut
singing and dancing
religious questions

gasping he turned right a figure of
ate the English reel, sentiment
simply suppression of difference

3.

in tent city the rain never stopped

the north wound up their windows

following a process of implantation the people
grew genetically frail my exploration of their
frozen culture took some time I took the long
way round got in through the back pulling
down the shades it was a premiere site

I couldn't keep up the pace
mass eviction behind
the lines and because of
desertion they set up cells

bees moved back and forth

positioned across the saddle with both
feet on the floor I felt the ground tremble
my mosquito net full to the brim
his anger management

4.

lens go pixellate barely awake
I cannot foresee scattered
boulder matter
or where air came from
hoping for some improvement
behind the fly wire keeping
the exits clear beyond the pale

5.

it was nightly
against the dark sky figure becomes ground
I associate with maps
monsoon weather
landscape
no escape
every day a different island
accustomed to humans
the steady chop of deforestation
and all I can do is repeat
across the road etc
to the river etc
between the flags of Ulster
on the banks of Mourne
a belief in new poverty
framed by the river they
work in arch enemies
as the money passed me by
the river curved him round

6.

I walked I was flagged down
caught red-handed Ulster
is a mist before the eyes
air between the upper limits
registered roads unclassified
byways to go the money to stay

he phoned home but
his number was up

7.

from O'Che's place deep in the
Galway jungle dogs bark
rolling out the lines of a lifetime

I asked again – how are you
she turned away and looked down
she ran her fingers across the table
she plucked at the spot on her chin

let's talk about hair

sodden movements

8.

caught red-handed
biting to the nail
little conversation
from the peace dividend
I roll back the eyes
lift the lids, ferret
it was a cool way to be
bare above the knees

across the divide
into enemy territory
as if everything is ok
in my dry phase
then the rain came
the eating phase
brown autumn began to turn
my hands to myself
people do believe in the system
syntax all over the place

I swallow nervously cling to a wire
ripe fruits appear clustered on the branch
but out of reach
closure is inorganic

9.

across the excavated beds sand drifts
each excavated grain
returns and turned again

cut a cross section
articulated layers
speak volumes
the date of ploughing
the way turf is turned

from the details, pictures
from fragments of bone, bodies
it was how it was meant to be

this is not a state of the art
but sand moving between its selves
the bucket and spade
flash of the camera

why should it have been any way else
how could it have been any place else

10.

from the 7th century her hair remained swept
across her right shoulder and blonde

she got the alarm call, the sea knocking at her casket
late for an appointment she had no choice but to

go out as she was, squinting into the mirror
embedded in the sun visor, before the bob, the

undercut the Mohican, she would have
walked the strand at Trearddur, waiting for the ferry

Lights

the sun boiled and sputtered
behind the ridge
pools go magenta
the ridges in the sand

and unfolding
within the line's dance
beyond the bright undercurrent
I hear mud rustle
ducks come in to land
tide recedes in intensity

blood filled hands
I mean lands
the duck glides
and lands

From 'turning out the way I am'

1.
on the jib of a crane
– Dylan Thomas –
everyone taking their time
as if it was theirs to take
calculating their power of purchase
hanging on by their fingernails
realising at the last minute
and stalking the perimeter of a burnt out building
the last charred spars finally lifted free
hanging in the air
make a window on the world
and how much was that
levered free from its fixings

2.
with a border drawn round them the paw marks of a big dog
skidding to a halt in the sand become a vase of flowers
flocks of terns fluttering in to land against a dark hill
onto pale sand over and over the bend of estuary

3.
the dividing line between encircling the contours of the hills
or going native down the valley
is a slipped word in the wrong place
and I can get emotion by repetition I can if all else fails me
or emphases at the synapse

4.
circling like dogs the gods of war
the lyric eye at the head of the stairs
a sight for sore eyes

the sun breaking up clouds
everything atrophied
persistently refuse

he constructed his characters with extreme care and then
crumbling into ash in the heat of the moment
conversation at a range of layers
within the wherewithal
four bedrooms, two receptions, the usual offices

flying around the place can make for a feeling of self-importance
he strolled the garden
his hands clasped behind his back the imaginary coat tails
like an amputated limb
a site for sore eyes lined up like marbles he peered

he was an allusion, a figment of an overwrought imagination
by following in the footsteps of others he caught cold
turned back and began to copy out page upon page
until his extremities, starved of blood by excessive smoking, shrank
to a quarter their original size. sure it's a process of rowing back and forth
peering into the still waters and waiting until the cat's paws
come rippling across the surface

5.
I began with a negative and its strap line to the metal shell
from the completed circuit
a charge leaks into churned earth and is discharged

I am up to my knees in it
each generation makes the idle promise
of clarity and coherence the flesh
cut into coordinates a compass
embedded in the navel its needle
reckons due east I pack

and fit my fingers into shapes so familiar that the borders blur
I sit in the corner of an empty house and dream in short bursts whatever
his good intentions scattered in a pile of trash
poking about in the dark cellars of his mind
he came up with death watch beetle wet rot

on the other hand

shapes emerged which were
down trodden and washed smooth
their origins undetectable

As if Only

The alley way – Barcelona 2004

I understand compulsion

limbs simply carriers for veins

I comprehend obsession

discarded at the first sign of infection

I appreciate anxiety

ways of fixing things for the present

it is a sick joke to make the body most
receptive to things that will kill it

condemned to distraction
compensation
I mean the throw of the dice
I mean never say die
never say the same thing twice

in bog myrtle

(for Lee Harwood)

sighted down the broken wall to where
a series of valleys from the ridges at the
heads of the valleys agencies

I overlooks
I views
I sights
an aim in life

mountain stand and deliver
before setting off again, swinging a trail leg
the angles were kind of cute
lunch simply
pause between breaths

they should wait until the pears drop or the
orchard reaching out to another in the
silence inhabitants
used lights
as indicators
and could turn either way
eyes might dim
or the advantage point sink without a trace

the sounds rustled across the plain
swept the surface of the lake
as haw and
blackthorn twisted
which trunk was
which myths circulated

standing before the tree and wondering
which sloe or haw
staring down the valley
drawing a line
points of view
the things that get told
you got me there

No Way Back

Sun shifts position
wind from another
quarter blockages
the movement of water
concentration poor or off centre
heart turned over love and
sex the worn rock undercut
a wash from the west

There is no second chance only the
rearrangement of the senses the
pull of the heart sings discordant
across the generations of the things that
move us most; bone, muscle, blood
the desire for the perception
of beauty the desire for the
attainment of beauty

There is no second wind
air moving past or the blow
to the head and catch as catch can
a few words clutched beyond the
point of no return he turns and
disappears as a figure of speech
points to the horizon look at
that

I compose myself a series of
crotchets minims things I could
well do without membership
expired and the aspiration
to fulfil the task of a
better world I arrange
organs of speech clear my
throat begin to say something

The sea drags shingle
over and over the stone in
heaps of stone more smooth
granite pebbles more marble
and what can politics tell me
of the soft landscape
of the body or the hard wiring
of sex or what can landscape

Tell me of the soft politics
of the body of the first
fix the performed
operation as the
memory of a warm body etched
in the soft tissue as it drips
word by word as it
tears itself sentence by

Sentence as it storms
image through dirty image and
the arguments go on in a parody
of logic as if the answer is
buried in the disorganisation
as if once the bits and pieces
of the past are finally slotted
into place or maybe the

Unexamined life is the better
option or the air from an open
window and what can
intelligence tell me I don't
already know as if the tips of
the fingers or the mobile lips
could lie and in confidence here's
the lines from around my eyes

From staring at the setting sun
from a westerly coast where
the rocks in layers lower themselves
into the sea and the guillemots
come and the choughs flash their
legs or the puffins and I'm still
scared to go up high into the
lighthouse still and scared to look back

The Independent

When people in a tube train look
anxiously around at other people on a
tube train. When all the scraps
of litter have been cleared the discarded
bits and pieces of urban life. When the
scaffolding goes up and the
polythene sheets go round
and the journalists sit in a pen in the
middle of the road their cameras on tripods
just waiting and waiting. This is no time to
play with words. This is a time
for plain speaking.
Like these bombs are not connected
to the invasion of Iraq.
That's plain speaking.
That gets to the heart of the matter.
And I know in order to be clear
I have to tell lies or at least strip so
many of the difficulties away there is nothing
worth anything left as if the bare truth is no
truth at all and to get to the heart of the matter
is to discard all matter that matters and once the
difficulties in explaining almost anything
become the difficulty then that's when
the difficulty of the situation is explored.
See what I mean? This is hard.

A number of conflicting emotions
which refuse to consolidate.
Or even incomprehension.
That would be good. I cannot comprehend.
I wish I could say that and mean it. You cause
a war on someone's soil and then they bring
a bit of it back to yours. How hard is that to
comprehend? But then again, shrinking into

myself in a tube train. In that confined place
with all those people. How to speak plainly
of that or even think it in any way other
than in language that cannot contain it.

There is no position I can hold for more
than a moment and the wind from an
approaching train pushes me up and
out of the tube into the hot street
and the names of the streets and the
faces of the people and I cannot
take it all in or give it out.

There is no single perspective but on
bended knee or on all fours or the view
from above as if there is a thing called justice.
As if there might be neutral ground
from which this could be
understood or called to account or
any system or any due process or twelve
good men and true. The apostles bore witness.
The judge walks on water. A judgement is final.

between mess and message

walking the streets with a dead
bird cradled in his hands
not always fully dressed

he would arrange matches around the
bed to trip up any in
truders or dislocate mischief

makers he carried a hatchet on

special occasions

laying down in the road for no
apparent reason the
car went over him and killed him

it could be that quick
and for no apparent reason
so sudden and for no apparent
cause

they hung speakers from the upstairs
windows so they rattled the glass of
the flat below to drive him crazy

that was a slow process but effective

the random nature of sudden death
the slow progress of terminal illness
the accident of accident of nonsense
of mental illness that eats away at the
corners of the room and lets in anything

a world gone mad and where sense
flies out through the window there is

no sleep that can cure bad dreams
no cure for too many meaningless words

fish, flesh and fowl

Puffyn a fysshe lyke a teele

with its short wings
the puffin
is hardly a bird at all

Puffins, whom I may call the feathered fishes, are accounted even by the holy fatherhood of Cardinals to be no flesh but rather fish

it tastes of sand eels
is confused with the razor bill
the guillemot
the young shearwater

Puffins, Birdes less then Dukkes having grey Fethers like Dukkes

caught by a gust it can
rise like air the puffin
eaten during lent as a
matter of convenience

The Puffyn..whose young ones are thence ferretted out, being exceeding fat, kept salted, and reputed for fish, as comming neerest thereto in their taste

or a sort of Coot or Seagull, supposed to be so called from its round belly; as it were swelling and puffing out.

Known by the fishermen as sea parrots or coulternebs; but more generally designated in books as puffins.

the bill was neither
large nor coloured the key
identifier of a puffin as I tried
to weave a story like the
steps that wind inside the
lighthouse as the story rose

I have twenty lambs … as plump as puffins.

increasingly insecure
and feeling the vertigo of a
lack of accuracy there
were spots of rain an island
view the setting sun

under cloud cover I leant
on the bar talked about
myself a subject as
constructed as if there is no
relationship between the words
and anything else as a puffin
turns out to be a guillemot or a
razor bill or a bird is a fish for lent

and what is in the name whether
the short bird puffs to itself at the
speed of its wings or its puffed
out beak a delicacy and tasting
of the fish it lives on and the
puffing sound it makes a short
growl or laugh but all these are
unlikely conjecture and based
on insecure grounds

language can only take you so far
sometimes you have to step out
sometimes you have to quieten the
jangle of nerves connect the
inside and outside or link
skin onto skin the loose ends
of being alive and waiting for a
connection I went to the old places
and walked them around again

Partly in Riga

Dirty Money — The Riga Museum

On the shores of Doles island the reindeer hunters
their situated pursuits; fishing, hunting, things
they can touch before the abstraction of coinage

and its brutal control by enforced amputation.
The scales that calculated the weight of
every crime that gets between teeth, scales

falling from my eyes. The insides of an animal,
the liver of a fish, is cleaner than
dirty money passed from hand to hand.

Failures of the Christian missionaries brought crusaders.
The same the world over, rock and a hard place, devil or

deep blue sea, Russia or Germany. Madonna on a
crescent moon waning the national awakening

Skulte and Saulkrasti

On the train line north of Riga. A line of
sand dunes topped with scots pine, birch and
rowan and a grey Baltic whipped into small
waves. what the fisherman in their small
inflatables saw as they stood around with their
backs to the wind much longer than was necessary
to discuss their catch. The left hand uncertain
as to what the right was doing
and just beyond their line of vision.
The next day thunder
rumbled in the background, rolling around the city,
the climate out of control
the heating boiler set to zero a heavy shower

forecast and all for nothing. We were wet, dripping,
leaking through the boundaries, hands breaking
through the surface of the sea cross hatched
and a line of waves breaking along the
shore. My back was a windbreak to fine
sand whipped up by a stiff breeze and a face
turned upward to a grey sky and a trawler turning to
show its length and the surface of the sea folding
over events as they unfolded as if nothing happened.

Dear Diary

Dear Diary On a gangway of a million shiny belt buckles; a conveyor belt going east. I am a travel agent; take off my uniform and try to imagine. There is only so much experience, the rest is supposition, the blocked out section beyond the tracks where vertical and horizontal combine until the place I'm in becomes a picture of the place I'm in. I've never been there and relationships may not be immediately evident.

Dear Diary Near the mouth of a river and up against the wall I learn to say certain words as a form of preparation. How much help will it be?

Dear Diary Your pages are stuck together with language like glue; they are plastered against the wall; a wall as tall as gravity permits in a surface that defies aspiration, sucking in the money. It is sticky with the heat of excitement and dripping onto the paving below.

Dear Diary I believe every word you say. Your handshake is dry and the words rustle as I walk through them, kicking them aside to reveal a pathway beneath, your skin has none of the usual signs of anxiety.

Dear Diary Melene from Strasbourg was an expert in Ai Kido and student of all things Japanese. I explained the principles of poetic composition to her. I was never good with girls. She asked me to write her haiku, I had forgotten how to count. She was a collector, her sketch book full of badly drawn faces of people she barely knew. When we embraced briefly in the European way to say farewell at a railway station some miles from here, her skin was unfeasibly soft.

Dear Diary I am reduced to waveforms, patterns of sound and light, as I bob to another diary entry sucking the end of my pen. Verticals have become horizontal simply by tilting my head. The relationship of a city to the coast is not always immediate. Spat out of the mouth of the river an urban sprawl often spreads between banks. This one does.

Dear Diary My method is more than technique. A trick off the wrist. I'm never sure I'll get out alive, twisting at the end of the line, turning into a siding, resting up, hitting the buffers.

Dear Diary I believe in concrete. Where the con is the series of inner stresses that will blow it apart and a lack of integrity that bubbles across the surface.

Dear Diary I am impatient for you to fill, although I believe in you and your waiting page.

Dear Diary In the opera house I saw a ballet with the dancers dressed in army uniform. Or peasant outfits. They seemed satisfied with themselves and were very skilled, making fantastic shapes with their bodies. If there was a narrative it was either too subtle or too banal to follow. It was impossible to order a drink; the system was simply too complex. It was my first trip to the ballet.

Dear Diary I'm letting you down and engaging in other activities without telling you. I'm not keeping you up to date. Things are just moving too quickly and there is a catch in my throat.

Dear Diary Two men with a video camera approach a young couple kissing on a riverbank. They are asked to kiss while being filmed, and then leave with the two men. I express concern in various ways; verbally, visually.

Dear Diary The construction of a national identity is a violent matter, bringing wealth to the military men, the signwriters, cartographers, publishers and historians. The reconstruction of a nation is a homely matter; the books on the shelves, the food we eat, where we bury our dead and how long they live. Ancient pathways, brushed aside, distant feelings, it will come to no good, a temporary resting place on the road to all's well.

Dear Diary It's all due to dual coding. Separately and together. Deeper waters than I can possible imagine and repeatedly crossed by the disappearing tracks of ships as the naturalised relationships between language, landscape, and the in between.

Dear Diary I fear your manipulations. As I occupied you it is now you who occupy me. I am putting you to the sword, denying you the words. I am is nothing and has little to say in the order things appear – one after the other.

Dear Diary This came next. Then this. By rearranging letters from *diagram* I can make *mad riga*.

Ways around the Llŷn

Ways around the Llŷn, as in
Matters of unchanged names paths
To a mountain top to the start
Point of chequered fields and the
Precise position of objects.

Ways around the Llŷn only lead
To other ways around
Llŷn, places are near and far
As distance is, relative
And familiar to other

Parts of the Llŷn. Between first
Cousin and second the family
Farm is uchaf or isaf.
The ways around the Llŷn can
Lead to Hell's Mouth from easy

Pasture to open moorland,
Gazing down at Llŷn heavens
Open. The arch bridges of Llŷn.
The way to hell is neither
Broad nor straight but winds around

Its stops, pick up points,
Or opportunities,
Chances to change direction
Or disembark, holding up
Pale hands, signalling, gestures.

Llŷn has little room for idle
Pedestrians winding their
Way home under a low moon,
Revealing the route to Hell's
Teeth beneath the surging waters

Of the Sound that span around
Settling little. The Sound is
On the way to hell. The Sound
Is a heavy swell, the sound
Beneath waves is of a bell

Clanging or an empty
Vessel without love beneath
The hollow sound of an empty
Heart. The Sound swells in different
Directions the surface of the

Sound Simultaneously
Peaks and troughs and, like a cork,
The Sound breaks on a rock my
Eardrums split a sound like an
Animal and like breathing.

On the landscaped surface
And on the way to anywhere,
Searching within ourselves for
Love in the Llŷn and overpriced
Parking, disinterested love

In the expensive fields.
Tired from the tramp of feet, blood
Singing in our ears from things outside
Things inside humming stuff
Stuff going on and coming

Off, blood, thicker than
Water inside the caverns of
A human heart its chambers
Washed by the morning tide
Scoured clean by the sound and every

Day the Llŷn cleaner the
Heart pumping with every upward
Step until blood, thicker than
Water across generations.
It was Easter and Passover

Or the fly past triple by
Pass or anyway my heart
Was surgically opened to
The wind around the headland
And uneven pathways leaning

Like a bent hawthorn arms at
Right angles. It appeared
Almost possible to fly
To transcend the cloudy
Sky, they are the politics

Of course of human love and
Best discovered at full tilt
And best forgotten in the
Effort to stay upright and
Best forgotten when recalled

In the night's Small Hours its
Little aches and pains the
Shape of the cross or almost
Ascension unobserved the
Teleport of G_d. It was

Easter so I walked the earth
Three long days skirting the
Jaw line of Hell's Mouth with its
Wet lips, the interactive earth
Where lights go off and on, the

Sun lays little eggs upon
The surface of the sea
And the chicks hatch chocolate.
Eggs melt in the mouth eyes water
In the wind the ways around Llŷn

That lead inward from leading
Outward from gazing down
And looking up from the dry
Surface of the earth in the
Rising wind and the high skies.

No Go Areas

With the surface of the word unfolding new connections occur
Previously impossible to imagine from sites of special interest
Where the next body politic will come from throwing themselves
At the exhaust smothering the world in sound from their insane
Silencers and the baroque ornament of LED lights systems
And stick on spoilers. Silver track suits.

That bunch of middle class kids called new labour are little threat
To the established order or the self interest of the self interested.
The revolutionary sixties a parody of itself in the over confident
Long haired children spat upon by hard faced remnants of the
Industrial working class. Maybe the unions did more than we
Thought possible. Maybe stay at home mothers held

Communities together rather than working all hours to get a
roof over their heads in moments of property madness.
Maybe our imaginations cannot contain whatever comes
Next or reveal the language folded into the
Words where beginning and end curl upwards to conceal the
Filling. Maybe what is hidden is never less than and always

Something more. Maybe the sound of revolution is the alloy
Wheels turning and the residual kindness of community.
Better the curled lip of those that never have all the fruit and
Veg they need or mothers fit to cook them than the overstuffed
Vitamin laden smoothies laced with condescension.
Within the nominal optimism of Chavez lies the word Chav.

I hope he will turn out ok and not sell his soul. Wearing sports gear
And smoking is ironic in the ways inside and outside coincide,
Smoke curling around the lungs and feeding the blood ridden
Veins and starving the brain of oxygen its subversive status
Assured by its new found illegality. The future is unimagined
But cancerous, a dark continent shadowing the breathing and

Where the past is an insecure guide who often gets it wrong.
The new revolutionary guard are of both sexes and impossible
To articulate and therefore temporarily safe from assimilation
At least until their video diaries make the news and spell out
A future. They require a disinclination to play any system and lie
Outside common sense in the flickering nature of humanity

Revealed by every shift in position or new relationships formed
Out of a shifting gaze. It is the law of the father the girls and boys
Fiddling with the bodywork of their little hatchbacks and
Challenging any sense of structural integrity and then
Going out to spit on the students or pink tracksuits or
Hair pulled back until tears come or escaping representation.

Beach Head

for elisabeth

Below a certain size rock
becomes sand or other
ornamentation. Below a certain
size plastic particles become

indistinguishable from sand.
Breached below the waterline
the shore becomes a container
for anything that might be lost,

a clutch bag for the
ornaments the world
discards, a necklace of rare
plastic objects to adorn its

skin or the dusting of
light that sparkles from
the surface scratched away
through exposure to salt water

and inorganic to the last. A
chair to stare out to sea
and watch the beach slowly
piling up into unidentified

particles of plastic nets and
the debris from the fishing left
as lace to hang from
the shoulder of a cliff

or an arm stuck out
across the sea or spit
of land between your eyes
with no way to disentangle

sand from plastic or
the ornamental. Sand
drifting; in the middle
of the ocean

a plastic lake, the
items rubbing up
against each other small
yellow ducks bobbing.

Things come together
then disintegrate. Things
are full of dread,
the world, in its best dress.

Appendix

Foreword to *Harsh*

For a while my work provided a laptop computer, and most nights I would come home, unpack the laptop, and write poetry. I hated my work but was in its grip. All my writing in this three-year period was in long pieces, often made up of short lines with only a couple of words in each. After a while I looked back over all the poetry I'd written in the previous three years and began to recycle what I considered to be the best of it into the fourteen line poems you find in this collection.

The sixth-century Chinese poet Wang Wei refers to the story of Chieh-yü, who feigned madness and lived as a recluse to avoid public service. On re-reading, the poems in the *HARSH* sequence seem to draw on the tensions of a public life that both provides the material and the impetus for the writing, and simultaneously robs the writer of the time and space for writing. In the poems there is the sense of a body that doesn't quite fit, a body that exists between rest and restlessness and between the endless spin of public affairs and a domestic life that both intrudes on and supports the writing.

Most of the writing was done while living amongst the mountains and the people of Eryri (Snowdonia). I was unprepared for the open minded generosity I encountered while living there, and can only put their free thinking down to living at an altitude some way above most administrative bodies. I thank them. Diolch yn fawr.

From the Foreword to *At a Stretch*

These poems were written using a variety of procedures; from a daily journal, from logs of specific journeys, from following the progress of a road being built, from archaeological digs and from the experience of a body producing space. Some are located in specific places but most move between places and some remain in between.

From the Introduction to *As if Only*

When the place runs out on you, rushing through the broadband, covered by the rising sea or receding to a distant memory, then the only place left is the body. So I turned back on myself and picked over the marks on my skin. I photographed myself from close up. I lost weight and put it back on. I started smoking again then gave it up, many times. So the poems are about the body, and its desire to communicate with others, whether through the rustle of skin or the tapping of the keyboard.

www.ingramcontent.com/pod-product-compliance
Lightning Source LLC
Chambersburg PA
CBHW031420160426
43196CB00008B/1000